12222

$18⁰⁰

DATE DUE

DRUGS, RUNAWAYS, AND TEEN PROSTITUTION

No matter how bad problems at home may seem, running away is never the right solution.

THE DRUG ABUSE PREVENTION LIBRARY

DRUGS, RUNAWAYS, AND TEEN PROSTITUTION

Clare Tattersall

THE ROSEN PUBLISHING GROUP, INC.
NEW YORK

Published in 1999 by The Rosen Publishing Group, Inc.
29 East 21st Street, New York, NY 10010

First Edition

Library of Congress Cataloging-in-Publication Data

Tattersall, Clare.
    Drugs, runaways, and teen prostitution / Clare
    Tattersall.
        p.   cm. — (The drug abuse prevention library)
    Includes bibliographical references and index.
    Summary: Explores the path from runaway to teen prostitute and examines the links between these activities and drug use among teenagers.
    ISBN 0-8239-2827-6
    1. Runaway teenagers—United States—Juvenile literature. 2. Teenagers—Drug use—United States. 3. Teenage prostitution—United States—Juvenile literature. 4. Drug abuse—United States—Prevention—Juvenile literature. [1. Runaways. 2. Prostitution. 3. Drug abuse.]   I. Title. II. Series
HV1431.T37   1999
362.74—dc21   98-400025
                                                                CIP
                                                                 AC

Manufactured in the United States of America

Contents

Introduction

"**I** wish I had known more about life out there on the streets before I ran away," says Marlena. "I was miserable at home. Mom used to beat me black and blue every day.

"'You're stupid! You're no good!' she would say, and she would hit me. She was always angry when she came home after going out at night. She would wake me up and make me clean the house from top to bottom, then she would say that I was lazy and stupid, and she would make me clean it again. Sometimes I was so tired that I would fall asleep at school.

"I stole some money and ran away from home when I was fourteen. But after a few days, the money ran out. Soon my problems at home were just replaced by problems on the street—and those were usually worse."

When you're a teenager, life seems full of 7
problems. Sometimes those problems can seem overwhelming, and you may feel alone. You think that you are the only person who feels this way and that nobody understands you.

It is true that no one person's problems are ever exactly the same as anyone else's. Maybe you are having problems at home with a violent, alcoholic, or drug-addicted parent. Maybe you are experiencing verbal or even sexual abuse. Maybe you feel unpopular at school; perhaps you are being bullied or picked on.

We all want to feel important, valued, and loved, and if you don't feel this way, you—like many others—may think of opting for drastic and dangerous solutions to your problems.

Some young people think about running away from home to escape their problems. To them, life away from the pressures of home and school sounds glamorous and fun. But life alone on the streets is anything but glamorous or fun. It is dangerous, ugly, and very hard to survive.

Some young people find themselves turning to prostitution—having sex or being involved in sexual activities in exchange for money. Teens may become involved in

8 prostitution either as a way to survive or as a way of trying to please others or feel loved. Ninety percent of teenage prostitutes are under the age of eighteen, and more than half of all teenage prostitutes start out as runaways.

Prostitution is illegal, and prostitutes can end up in jail. In addition, prostitutes are almost always involved with drugs. Some teens turn to prostitution to pay for a drug habit. Drugs are often used to lure young people into hustling (working as prostitutes). Whatever the route to prostitution, the result is almost always at least one, if not all, of the following:

- violence
- abuse
- illness
- self-hatred
- drug dependence or addiction

"I met a man named Troy, who was really good to me at first," recalls Marlena. "He bought me some new clothes and he took me to eat whenever I was hungry. He seemed so kind that I believed he was a good man and really cared about me. One day he asked me if I was happy. I said yes.

" 'You can make me happy, too,' he told me. I thought that sounded easy enough. Little did I know that my problems were about to begin."

Teens who are having trouble getting along with their parents may consider running away as a solution to their problems.

At first Marlena thought she was lucky. She had left a home where she felt rejected. The man she met seemed to want to take care of her. She felt good for the first time that she could remember. But this was only the start of her problems. Like many runaways, Marlena was about to experience the drugs, violence, and abuse that accompany teenage prostitution.

"I never thought this would happen to me," she says. *"I always thought that if I could just get away from that house and from Mom's yelling, then everything would be okay. I wish I had known then what I know now."*

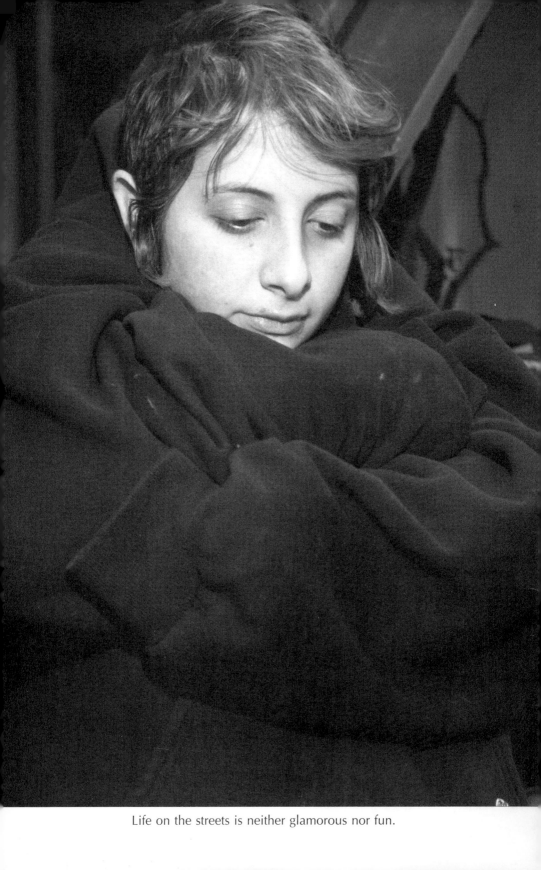

Life on the streets is neither glamorous nor fun.

CHAPTER 1

What is Teen Prostitution?

Who Becomes a Prostitute?

There is no particular type of person that will become a prostitute. There are no racial, religious, or ethnic groups that are more likely to be involved in prostitution than any other. But 40 percent of prostitutes are younger than eighteen years old, and young people are particularly vulnerable to being used in this type of work.

Boys can also be prostitutes. They are no less vulnerable than girls. In fact, the typical adolescent boy is easily sexually aroused, sexually curious, inexperienced, and rebellious, so in some ways boys are more easily seduced into prostitution. Nonetheless, more girls than boys become prostitutes.

12 There are two main reasons that teen-agers become involved in prostitution: the need for attention and the need for affection. These needs can be equally strong whether you are alone on the street or living at home.

The Need to Survive

Alone on the street, you are defenseless. If you've been having a hard time at home, being on your own may seem exciting at first. But what happens when the money runs out and you have nowhere to stay? Where do you go? Do you ride the subway all night just for a warm place to sleep? Do you huddle in doorways or sleep on a park bench?

What few teenagers think about before they run away is how to survive on their own. You may think that it is easy to find an apartment or get a job, but responsible adults will not rent an apartment to anyone who is under eighteen, and most of the jobs that teenagers are able to get do not pay enough for rent, food, and expenses. This leaves you as a perfect target for the pimps, perverts, and manipulators of society.

There are people out on the streets who are looking for young people like you. Some of them want to help. They may be volunteers who only want to offer you food, counseling, or a safe bed for the night. But far more common are the people who want to use you to make money for themselves. They are experts at finding impressionable young people. They know how to talk to you. They know the "in" games, toys, and TV shows. They know that you are lonely and looking for attention and affection.

"I had been sleeping on a park bench for three nights," says Marlena. "I was starving and cold and terrified. I didn't feel safe in the park, but I didn't know where else to go. I was just huddling down for the fourth night when this man came and sat down next to me. He started asking my name and where I came from and lots of questions. You always learn when you're a kid not to talk to strangers, but I was just too cold and hungry to care. He told me his name was Troy. He said he would buy me dinner if I wanted. I was so hungry that I would have done just about anything for a sandwich.

"We went for a burger. I ate three. Troy said that if I didn't want to go back to the bench in the park, I could stay at his house. I was starting to trust him. I stayed at his apartment. It was the best night's sleep ever. Over the next few days, he took me out to eat three times a day. He bought me a new pair of shoes and some clothes. No one had ever been this kind

14 *to me before. I felt important eating out and going shopping. He even brought me a pair of gold earrings one day. He made me feel special.*

"One day he asked me if I was happy. I said yes. He told me that I could make him happy too. I asked him what I had to do, and he said to just come to a party with him. I thought that sounded easy enough.

I had never been to an adult's party before, so I was feeling really grown up. He gave me a mirror with some powder on it and a rolled-up ten-dollar bill. He told me to snort the powder into my nose through the bill, and I did. I found out later that it was cocaine. I felt great. I felt pretty and special and happy. I was high.

"Later Troy told me to go into a room with one of his friends. As I was going in, I saw the other man hand Troy some money. In the room, the man started to undress me. I was fourteen and didn't really know what was happening, but I was so high on cocaine and I felt so good that I went along with it.

"That man took my virginity.

"The next day, I woke up and it was afternoon already. It gradually came back to me what had happened, and I felt so ashamed and miserable. I thought of running away from there too, but Troy had been so kind to me. When he came home he gave me a few dollars

Many runaways turn to drugs as a way of dealing with life on the streets.

16 *and said I had earned them. He asked me how I felt. I didn't want to tell him the truth, so I lied and said, 'Okay.' He told me that I could earn more money the same way, and if I did, he would let me stay in his apartment.*

"I had sex with a lot more men, and it was easier and easier each time. I felt numb and empty. I earned just two dollars for each man."

Ninety percent of teenage prostitutes are runaways, both male and female. Like Marlena, young people on the street need money, food, shelter, and love, and they may think that prostitution is the best way to get these things. But the truth is that being a prostitute means making a large amount of money for someone else, and leaving yourself poor, possibly addicted to drugs, and emotionally and physically bruised.

Pimps and Madams

Pimps are men who sell the services of prostitutes to clients, usually also men. Women who sell these services are called madams. Pimps and madams keep most or all of the money the prostitute earns. A pimp may have only one prostitute— perhaps even his girlfriend—working for him, or he may have a "stable," a whole group of prostitutes.

Pimps often approach teens in malls, bus stations, and other public places.

Pimps and madams are always on the lookout for young boys and girls who seem like likely targets. They search the malls, video arcades, bus stations—anywhere that young people hang out. They start conversations and ask questions about you and your interests. They may seem friendly, but they are really just finding out if you have an unfulfilled need.

They find out whether you are window-shopping for clothes that you can't afford; whether you are skipping school; whether you are bored with rules and restrictions at school or at home. They ask if you are popular, or if you have a boyfriend or girlfriend.

18

Then they use this information to make a connection with you. If you are tired of school rules, they tell you that you are too smart for all that. If you are lonely, they offer friendship. If you think you are unattractive, they flatter you. They might invite you to join them for a meal or a game in the video arcade. They will spend money on you and make you feel special, grown-up, interesting, wanted.

Tonya grew up in a nice suburban house in the Midwest. She was thirteen when she started skipping school. She started hanging out at the mall, window shopping and reading magazines. She thought that she was not pretty enough and that she would never have a boyfriend. For Tonya, going to school was a daily reminder that being smart was not enough; you had to be pretty to be popular.

One day a man started talking to her at the mall. He asked her why she wasn't at school. She told him that she hated school because the popular girls picked on her and laughed at her. The man told her his name was Mark. He told her she was too smart to worry about those silly girls at school anyway. "You're really pretty," he said. "Hasn't anyone ever told you that before?" No one had ever shown this much interest in her. Tonya and Mark strolled around the mall, checking out the clothes. He talked about music and bands. He seemed really knowledgeable and cool. Then he asked her if she wanted to meet him later so they could go to a party together.

Tonya met Mark later that evening. She slipped out of the house when her parents thought she was studying in her room. She met Mark as planned. He gave her a box, and inside was a dress that she had admired that afternoon. She ran into the restroom and changed into it. She felt surprised and excited. Mom and Dad would never let her wear anything like this. She thought she looked really cool. The dress was tight and red.

Tonya and Mark went to the party. Mark offered Tonya a joint to smoke. He gave her a shot of vodka, and then another. Tonya had never drunk alcohol before. After two drinks, she lost her ability to focus. Everything seemed to swim in front of her eyes. All she remembered was being dropped off at home before dawn so that no one would notice that she was missing.

Over the next few weeks, Tonya slipped out of her house at night and went to several parties. She was starting to feel like she really counted. People always told her how pretty she was, and the men gave her lots of attention. She was introduced to new drugs that made her feel powerful and attractive. She thought

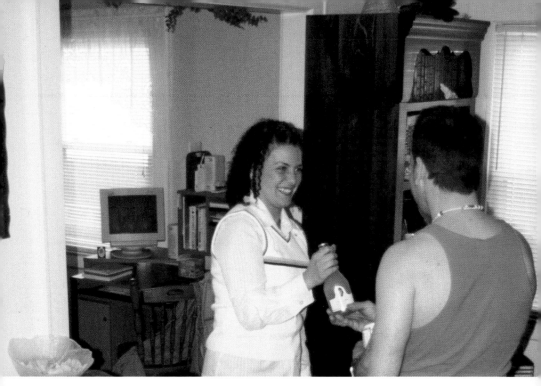

Pimps may use alcohol and drugs to help break down a teen's defenses and persuade them to engage in prostitution.

she was being very grown-up. As she became more dependent on the drugs to make her feel good, she went to school less and less often.

One day Tonya woke up sore and bruised after a night of heavy drug use at one of Mark's parties, and she did not know why. She was really scared that her mom would notice the bruises, but she covered them up with long-sleeved turtlenecks. The next time she met Mark at the mall, she asked him, "What happened to me?" She tried to treat it as a joke.

"I'll show you," he said. He took her to his house and showed her a video. The video showed her being gang-raped at the party by five men. Watching this, Tonya was stunned. She felt ashamed, humiliated, and degraded.

"Why did you do this?" she asked. But Mark just laughed at her. She did not know what to do. There was no one she could tell. Mark was her only friend.

Mark took her for a drive and pointed out some prostitutes on the streets. He told her that if she cared about him she would be a prostitute too. "Don't you care about me, after all I've done for you?" She began to think she owed it to him to become a prostitute.

Tonya was still living at home when she started turning tricks (having sex for money) for Mark. She became totally dependent on him. Her family did not realize what was happening when Tonya dropped out of school and moved out of their house. She moved in with Mark, who regularly beat her. She had such low self-esteem that she believed she deserved this treatment. Besides, Mark said he loved her. No man had ever told her that before.

The actress and sex symbol Marilyn Monroe once said, "A sex symbol becomes a thing," and that was how Marlena and Tonya felt—like things, not human beings.

Pornography

Pornography is a permanent record of sexual activity and exploitation. It can be in the form of photographs, videotapes,

22 | films, or magazines. Because it is a permanent record, not only is there damage to you at the time it is made, but it can also come back to haunt you later in life.

You do not have to be a runaway to be used in pornography. Many teens involved in it live at home and are seduced by someone they know, such as a family member, family friend, teacher, or clergyman. Runaways, however, are more likely than other young people to become prostitutes and to be involved in pornography.

Children who are taken into pornography suffer from depression and guilt. They grow up to feel that they have no worth and very often lead a life of drug abuse and prostitution. Children who are sexually abused are more likely to abuse children themselves when they are older.

CHAPTER 2

The Dangers of Teen Prostitution

Most prostitutes have been victims of violence by either their customers or their pimps.

Simon, a fifteen-year-old male prostitute from Texas, says, "I was repeatedly beaten up by johns. Twice I was taken to a field, raped at knifepoint, and kicked so badly that I couldn't work for days afterwards. I was often beaten up by johns who tried to get their money back after the act and I have been raped I don't know how many times."

The relationship between the pimp and the prostitute is based on abuse—sexual abuse, drug abuse, physical abuse, and financial abuse. Pimps need the money that

24 prostitutes work hard to earn, and they will go to any lengths to make sure that you keep earning that money for them.

There are many dangers involved in prostitution—dangers that may threaten or destroy your life. Many prostitutes claim that they "sold their souls," that they have no dignity left, that they feel worthless, and that they cannot believe in tomorrow because tomorrow might never come. Female prostitutes make up 5 percent of the total number of women murdered each year. Prostitutes are frequently the victims of serial killers who believe that they are "cleaning up society."

Drugs

Many of the hard times that prostitutes have to deal with are related to drug addiction. Most young prostitutes say that they did not choose prostitution as a way of earning money but were forced into it. Many young people become involved after being introduced to drugs (as Marlena and Tonya did) or to support their drug habit. Most teenage prostitutes say that they use drugs or alcohol as part of their lifestyle, and many of them say that they are addicted—that they have a physical or psychological need for drugs.

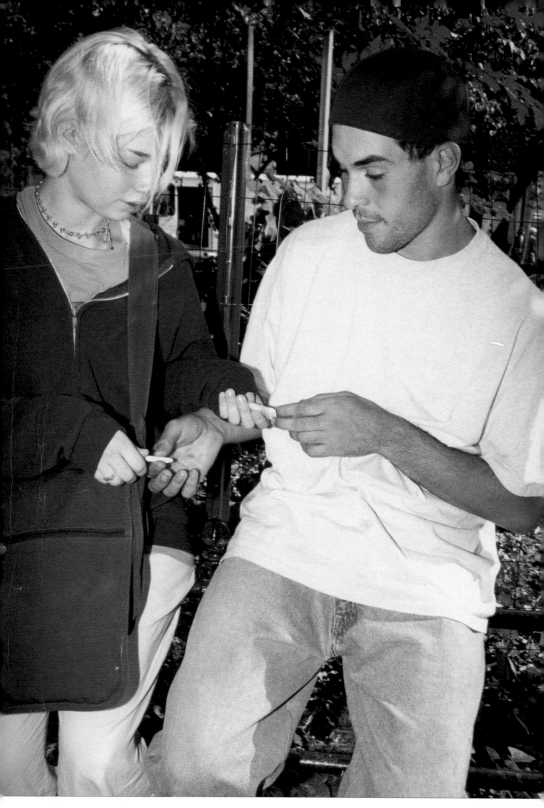

Runaways often turn to prostitution as a way to support their drug habits.

26 Many prostitutes abuse drugs as a way of dealing with the pain and humiliation of prostitution. Prostitutes who become addicted to drugs find it hard to change their lifestyles, because they need the quick money to support their drug habits.

Prostitutes may use any of several different types of drugs, both legal and illegal.

Alcohol

Alcohol depresses some of the brain's functions; it slows down your ability to think and react. Heavy drinking can make you lose consciousness, and long-term use damages your body, particularly the liver.

Heroin

Heroin is one of the most addictive of all drugs. It can be smoked, injected, or snorted. Long-term heroin use reduces the user's energy and sex drive and destroys the motivation to do anything except get the next dose, or "fix." Over time, heroin does severe damage to the body's systems and is often fatal. In one study, 96 percent of street prostitutes said that they used heroin regularly, and 84 percent said they were addicted.

Speed

Methamphetamine, usually called speed, gives you a rush of energy, but when it wears off, you are left exhausted and depressed. It can also make you behave irrationally. Continued use will seriously damage your mind and body and can be fatal.

Cocaine and Crack

Cocaine gives you a short but intense high and a feeling of power. It is very addictive and can cause paranoia, the belief that others are out to get you. You can inject or snort cocaine in powder form. It can also be mixed with chemicals to return it to its base form and then smoked. This is known as "freebasing," and it is very dangerous because of the chemicals involved.

Crack, or rock cocaine, is a cheap form of freebase cocaine. It produces a more powerful high and is even more addictive than cocaine. It can cause severe lung damage, violent behavior, and death.

Marijuana

Marijuana is smoked in cigarette paper or in a pipe. It affects perception and coordination and slows down your reactions. Over time it can cause paranoia and depression.

LSD

LSD radically changes your perception and distorts reality so that you hallucinate—you hear or see things that don't exist. LSD is

28 swallowed. It can cause very bad "trips" which are frightening and can lead to depression and brain damage.

Inhalants

Inhalants include glue, gasoline, lighter fluid, typewriter correction fluid, and other products that are readily available around the house or at the store. They tend to give you a quick high. The side effects are vomiting, dizziness, and headaches. In the long term, inhalant use can lead to heart failure, brain damage, and sudden death.

Other Health Risks

In addition to the dangers of drug abuse, prostitutes also face daily risks such as illness, pregnancy, and violence.

STDs and AIDS

Sexually transmitted diseases, or STDs, are the best-known illnesses associated with prostitution. STDs include diseases such as herpes, gonorrhea, and hepatitis B, as well as human immunovirus (HIV) and acquired immunodeficiency syndrome (AIDS). Between one-half and two-thirds of teenage prostitutes get STDs from their work because they are too young to know about the diseases, and 30 percent of teenagers use no precautions against them.

Even in brothels (places where groups of prostitutes offer their services) where the girls use condoms and are given regular check-ups, 10 percent of the workers become infected each week. Pimps and madams usually keep their prostitutes away from doctors and family-planning clinics because they are afraid of authorities who might interfere with their illegal activities.

The introduction of HIV and AIDS to the world has brought terrifying new risks to prostitutes. AIDS can be sexually transmitted through bodily fluids from men to men, men to women, women to women, and women to men. Anyone who has sex can get it; it is not just gay men or drug abusers who are at risk.

The younger a teen prostitute is, the more likely he or she is to be infected, because he or she does not know how to prevent catching the disease or how to reject johns (men who use prostitutes for sex) who are infected. Most teen prostitutes either don't know how to get medical help or are prevented from getting it. The younger you are, the less control you have over your situation, and consequently, the greater your risk.

Teenage boys are at greater risk for AIDS than teenage girls, but both male and

30 female prostitutes are at a far higher risk than other teenagers. Consistent use of condoms can reduce the risk of infection, but there is no such thing as "safe sex." In a recent survey of prostitutes in seven cities, 108 of 835 prostitutes tested positive for HIV, and only 4 percent said that they regularly used condoms.

Teenage prostitutes are at risk for a number of other health problems. Male hustlers are likely to have injuries to the rectum if they have anal sex with johns. Both boys and girls can easily pick up hepatitis or other serious diseases that are not common among other teenagers. Prostitutes' lives are stressful, and stress makes people more susceptible to illness. In addition, prostitutes rarely eat properly or wear enough clothes to keep warm and healthy.

Pregnancy
Half of all prostitutes under the age of twenty have been pregnant once already, and 20 percent have been pregnant twice or more. Teenagers who are prostitutes do not have safe places in which to be mothers. They do not have enough money to raise a child. Research shows that their babies are neglected. The financial and

Teen prostitutes are frequently assaulted by their pimps or customers.

psychological difficulties that prostitutes have already are doubled by the responsibilities of having and raising a baby.

Suicide

Suicide is a serious health risk for teen prostitutes. Thirty-nine percent of boys and 68 percent of girls involved in prostitution have attempted suicide. Teenage prostitutes try to commit suicide because they are deeply depressed. One study found that almost all the female prostitutes surveyed thought that they had no other option in life but to sell their bodies.

Violence

Pimps will use physical or psychological violence against you to make sure that you

32 do not leave them. There are two important reasons that they don't want you to leave. First, they do not earn money on their own, so they need you to make money for them. Second, they are afraid that you will report them to the police or other authorities.

Once pimps have lured you into their lifestyles, they will do whatever it takes to keep you there.

"Sex is not love," says Marlena. "It is like a drug. It promises you everything, but leaves you with nothing, sad and empty.

"I stayed with Troy for a long time. I thought he was my only friend, even though he beat me. I often went to work covered in bruises with two black eyes. He took almost all the money I earned. If I ever asked for more money, he would hit me and tell me I was ungrateful—that he gave me everything that I needed. A few times I wanted to leave, but he just laughed at me. That was one of the worst feelings. He laughed and told me that I could never do any other kind of job. He asked me what else I thought I was good for."

CHAPTER 3

Questions of Sexuality

"*I*'m gay," says Simon. "*My parents are very strict Christians, and I remember they would always say how evil gays and lesbians were, how they were rebelling against God's natural order. I felt ashamed and confused. I thought that I was different—that I was evil.*

"*I felt like I was about to explode. I wanted to talk to someone, but I was too afraid. I started to rebel at school and at home. I acted bad because I was angry, frustrated, and confused. One day I just decided that I couldn't take it anymore. I had heard about a place in Los Angeles where boys like me hung out.*

"*I wanted to get away from myself, really, not my family, but I hitched a ride from Houston to Los Angeles in search of people who would understand me and love me for who I am.*"

Nobody ever said growing up was easy. Your body and your emotions are changing. You want more independence, but your parents seem to suddenly create more rules. You don't feel popular at school. Maybe someone is making fun of you or picking on you. If you think you might be gay, or if others do, you may be called "faggot" or other names.

A well-known study of sexuality found that among teenagers, 28 percent of boys and 17 percent of girls have had at least one homosexual experience. This is not weird or abnormal. Some people try it and find that it feels right; other people try it and realize that it is not for them.

Being a teenager is hard, and being a gay, lesbian, or bisexual teen is even harder. Half of all gay and lesbian youths say that they have been rejected by their families because of their sexual orientation, which helps explain why 35 to 40 percent of runaways are gay or lesbian.

Eighty percent of lesbian, gay, and bisexual teenagers say that they feel isolated. They feel that they have no one to talk to or feel close to. They don't know where to go for advice or support.

Isolation is not only a cause of running away from home, it also turns some young

Some gay and lesbian teens are comfortable with their sexuality and are proud to be gay. Others are not as lucky.

people to drug and alcohol abuse. Thirty-one percent of gay teens and 18 percent of lesbian teens say that they abuse drugs to the greatest possible extent. In some tragic cases, the isolation and loneliness of being a gay or lesbian teen leads to suicide; 33 percent of teenagers who commit suicide each year are gay or lesbian.

Pornography and Prostitution

Child pornography shows children being used in both heterosexual and homosexual activities with adults or other children. Although there are laws against most forms of child pornography, it is still a big business. It makes a huge amount of money for the adults who run it. But the children

Pimps may film or photograph teen prostitutes having sex, then sell the videos or photos to customers.

are just victims, left with nothing but physical and psychological problems.

Drugs also play a central role in pornography. Many young people who are forced to appear in pornographic videos perform in exchange for drugs. Often they are so heavily drugged while the video is being made that they have no control over what they are being made to do. Most teenage prostitutes are used for pornography at some time, by their pimps or by johns.

"I didn't dare to disagree with anything Troy told me to do," says Marlena, "because I was afraid that he would take his attention away from me and I would be alone again. I never thought that being alone would be better than being humiliated and degraded."

Troy sometimes filmed Marlena when she was with customers. He also asked her to perform sexual acts with other boys and girls for the camera.

"I think he sold those movies that he made," says Marlena. "I cringe to think where they are now. I never know if they are going to come back to haunt me one day.

"I don't think I'm a lesbian, or even bisexual," she says. "I have had sex with other women. But I don't know what I think about that. I mean, I was so high on cocaine at the

38 | *time, and so willing to do anything that Troy asked me, that I didn't really have a choice."*

You do not have to be a runaway to be forced into pornography. But because runaways are more likely to become prostitutes, they are also more likely to be forced into pornography.

When pimps are on the lookout for young people, they are not concerned with sexual orientation. Male prostitutes, in particular, have to perform both heterosexual and homosexual acts, regardless of their own preference. Both girls and boys who are prostitutes are likely to get involved in straight and gay pornography whether or not they are gay themselves. They also risk having to deny their own sexuality.

Simon now lives on the streets making money the only way that he knows how. He is what is known as a "chicken"—an underage male prostitute. Most of his customers are male, but he will go with anyone who pays him, just to be able to earn enough money to eat. One day he was picked up and taken to a parking lot by a "chicken hawk," a john who uses underage male prostitutes.

"When we got to the parking lot, I did what he wanted. When we were finished, he tried to

get back in his car. He was going to drive off
*without paying me. I said, 'Hey, you owe me
for that.' He was a real rich, smug dude. He
just turned to me and said, 'I'm not paying you
for anything, you little faggot.'*

"I really lost it. It wasn't just that he didn't
want to pay me. That was bad enough, but cut
out the insults, I do what I have to do to
survive. I pulled him backwards out of his car
and punched him and punched him. I stole his
wallet and ran off. I got caught, of course. I was
picked up by the cops and I still had his wallet
on me. I'm paying for it now."

CHAPTER 4

Knowing The Rules

*S*imon *was picked up by a cop who was posing as a john. When Simon got in the car, he was arrested. He was taken to the police station and searched. They found the man's wallet on him. Simon was kept in detention over the weekend.*

"It was the worst," he said. "I never want to go back in there again." Simon spent the weekend in the detention center before he was charged on Monday with prostitution, aggravated assault, and theft.

Prostitution is illegal. Prostitutes can be arrested, taken to court, and either fined or put in jail. Being a teenager does not make a difference, as it does with some other crimes. In all except a handful of

states, teenage prostitutes are given the
same penalties as adults.

The use and sale of drugs in prostitution is also criminal, and drug-related crimes carry much more severe penalties than prostitution alone. Young prostitutes are also often arrested for robbery and assault. Many teenagers admit that they steal from their customers as often as possible. Boys in particular are often arrested for assault if they fight back when johns attack them. In some extreme cases, the difficulty of their situation and the sense that they have no way out of it have led some prostitutes to commit murder.

Pressure

When you are a teenager there is a lot of pressure on you to have sex. Television and movies show sex as an attractive choice. Friends put pressure on you. Boyfriends or girlfriends try to pressure you into having sex. People you meet may flatter you in a way no one else ever has. They may threaten to leave you if you do not have sex with them. Some answers that you can give when faced with this kind of pressure are:

- "I'm not sure yet, I want to wait."
- "If you care about me, you'll wait."

42

- "I don't think I'm ready yet."
- "It's against my religion."

Not giving in to pressure is the sign of a strong, independent person. Knowing your own mind and sticking with your decisions is a very attractive, admirable quality. When you give in to pressure, you are doing something because someone else wants you to, not because it is right for you.

Protection

There is no such thing as safe sex, but you can reduce the risk of catching AIDS and other STDs or becoming pregnant by taking precautions. What can you do to protect yourself?

- Say no. If you wait until you are older before you have sex you not only will enjoy it more, but you will be able to make better judgments.
- Limit your partners. Having sex with many people puts you at very high risk for unwanted pregnancy as well as AIDS and other STDs.
- Avoid high-risk partners. People at high risk include drug users and people who have multiple partners.

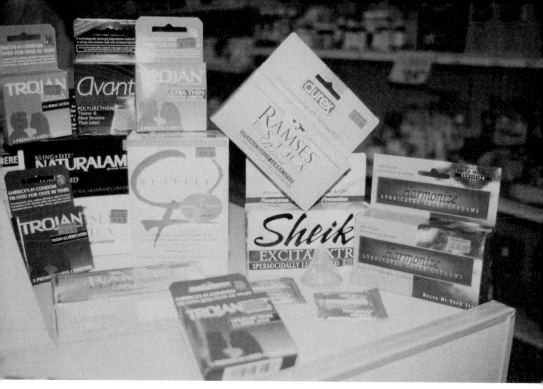

When used correctly, condoms can protect against the spread of AIDS and other STDs.

- Use condoms. Consistent use of condoms has been shown to reduce the risk of AIDS and to help protect against pregnancy.

What Do Condoms Do?

Condoms do not make sex completely safe, but they do make it safer. They can break or leak, but they are very important in reducing the spread of AIDS and other STDs.

Where Do You Get Condoms?

Condoms can be bought at any drugstore. You do not need a prescription, and you can buy them no matter how old you are. You may also be able to get them from school, from a family-planning clinic, or

44 from an AIDS information center. If you do not use a condom even once, you are playing Russian roulette with your life.

Important Points About Condoms

- Always use latex condoms.
- Never re-use a condom.
- Stop if you feel the condom break or fall off.
- Handle condoms carefully. They are easily torn by teeth, nails, and rings. Broken or damaged condoms are not effective.
- Use the condom at the start of sex and keep it on until the end.

There are other forms of birth control, such as the pill, the diaphragm, and the IUD (intrauterine device), which are available from a doctor or a family planning clinic. They all help protect against pregnancy but offer no protection against AIDS. All can be used in addition to condoms. Different forms of contraceptives suit the lifestyles of different people. Consult your doctor or clinic to find out which is best for you.

CHAPTER 5

Finding Help

It's important to remember that no matter how bad your problems may seem, running away will always make them worse. Instead of running away, try to find help in dealing with your problems. Asking for help with problems and difficult situations might be the most important thing you'll ever do.

If You're Thinking of Running Away

Running away might seem like the answer to your problems at home, but it isn't. Life on the street is very difficult, and you are only replacing the old problems with new, often worse ones. Running away does not solve anything.

When you want to deal with a problem, you need to determine what it is before you

46 | can deal with it. Here are some steps you can take to figure out your problem.

1. Write down exactly what is making you unhappy. It may be one thing or it may be many, but writing it down will make it clearer to you.
2. When you know what is making you unhappy, write down how you would like to change it. What would be your ideal alternative?
3. Decide who you would like to tell. Why do you want to tell this person? Do you trust them? Can they help you? What would you like them to do to help you?
4. Try talking to this person. Now that you know what you want to tell them and how you want them to help you, it will be easier for them to understand and help you.

It's Okay to Ask for Help

As a young person, you are not yet well equipped to deal with the problems that you are facing, even though you are trying your best. There are organizations, groups, and individuals who can help you find the best solutions to your problems.

Don't try to cope on your own. There

There are many free hotlines that specialize in helping teen runaways and prostitutes who want to find a better way to live.

are special hotlines and support groups for the issues that you are dealing with. Not all of these places will have all the answers that you need, but most will put you in touch with someone who can help you.

Do not be afraid to tell someone what is happening, but make sure that the person you tell is someone you can trust. Telling someone you trust probably won't end your worries immediately, but it could be the start of a solution.

Help with Problems at School

At most schools, there are counselors and peer counselors available. They will be glad to discuss your concerns. If you have a teacher you feel comfortable with, ask him

48 or her to listen to you. Teachers and counselors are used to hearing about problems.
Nothing will seem too big or too small, and
nothing is likely to surprise or shock them.
If they do not know how to help you, ask
them who you should talk to next.

Help with Problems at Home
Many young people choose to run away
because they are unhappy at home for any
number of reasons, including the following.

> **Rules** Some parents seem very
> strict. They may set extra rules
> because they want the best for you. It
> is their job to protect you. Try talking
> to your parents and tell them that
> you want more freedom. Show them
> that you are capable of being more
> responsible and independent. If they
> know they can trust you, they will
> probably be more understanding.

> **Divorce** When parents split up and
> find new partners, it is hard on you.
> Sometimes parents are so concerned
> with their own unhappiness that they
> do not notice yours. Talk to them.
> Tell them that you love them and
> would like to help them in any way

you can. Avoid taking sides. If you feel neglected, suggest ways that you can spend more time together. If your parents have found new partners, it may seem as if they have stopped caring about you. This is not the case. Sometimes adults become focused on themselves, but it does not take much to remind them that you need attention too.

Fighting Seeing your parents fight is painful, but remember that the fights are about them and not about you. Try not to get involved or take sides. If you need to get away for a little while, stay at a friend's house, but make sure you let your parents know where you are. Many family problems stem from bad communication. Talking to a counselor, as a family, often helps. Ask your school counselor for suggestions about how to approach your parents.

Alcohol or Drug Abuse If your parents are abusing drugs or alcohol, they need help. Alcoholics and drug abusers often deny that they have a problem. Confronting them about

50

their abuse is a delicate process.
Enlist the help of a trusted adult, but
remember that alcoholics and drug
abusers are very secretive and do not
want other people to know about
their problem. A counselor will be
able to help you decide whether to
confront your parent about the
problem and will help you find other
ways to deal with it.

Physical or Sexual Abuse. There is
no reason to accept abuse from
anyone. If you are being physically or
sexually abused, report it immediately. If someone is abusing you, they
are probably also making you feel
guilty for it or threatening that if you
tell anyone, you will break up the
family. Remember, you have done
nothing wrong; it is the abuser who
has. Get the help of someone you
trust as soon as you can.

While some of your problems can be
solved by talking to someone you trust and
enlisting their help, not all family problems
and situations can be cured so easily. If you
are living in a situation that is harmful to
you, a teacher, counselor, or social worker

can help you find an alternative. This may **51**
mean living with a relative or even in a
foster family. But there are also special
homes and programs for teens who are not
safe living at home.

Help with Drug or Alcohol Problems

Taking or selling drugs or drinking alcohol
may seem cool, but it isn't. Drugs and
alcohol will ruin any chance you have of
living a fulfilling life. If you are abusing
drugs or alcohol and are thinking of
running away, your fears and your addiction will only get worse. Tell someone
about your problem. Talking to your
parents is usually the best idea. They may
be scared and angry at first, but if you can
tell them that you need their help, then they
should realize that you are responsible and
serious about helping yourself. If you don't
feel that you can tell your parents, tell
another adult that you trust.

Help with Pregnancy

For reasons of religion or culture, some
parents will not be understanding if you are
pregnant. But running away and living on
the streets is not a solution either. Enlist the
help of someone else—for example another
relative, a teacher, a counselor, or a friend's
parent. When you are pregnant, you need

52 medical care for you and your baby. Running away will risk both of your lives.

What To Do If You Are On The Street

Life on the street is brutal, but it is also difficult to escape from. When you have been raped and beaten, when you have hustled for your hard-earned money that went straight into someone else's pocket, when you have injected, snorted, or smoked drugs just to get through the day, it is hard to believe in yourself or to believe that there is a better life that you deserve. But there are people and groups waiting to help you and others in your position.

If you want to contact someone at home, you can call a runaway hotline. The people who answer the phone will pass on messages without giving away any more information. They will also listen to you, direct you to the nearest shelter, and help you with any information that you need.

Whether you are thinking of running away or you are already on the streets, there are plenty of people and organizations that are designed especially to help you. They include the following.

- Covenant House is a worldwide organization. The people there can

Organizations such as Covenant House have volunteers who look for teens on the streets who need help.

offer you shelter, education, food, support, medical help and crisis counseling. Covenant House also runs an outreach program in many cities that offers food, warm clothes, and advice for teenagers who are not yet ready to come in off the streets. They also run a hotline that you can call at any time, as do several other organizations.

- Religious and nonreligious centers in many major cities offer free food and often clothing to the homeless.
- Gay and lesbian community centers, which are found in most large cities, can offer you specific

54

advice on dealing with sexuality. There are also some organizations, like the Hetrick-Martin Institute in New York, that cater to gay, lesbian, bisexual, and transsexual youths. The Hetrick-Martin Institute offers an alternative school, a drop-in center, shelter, food, and youth groups. Other gay and lesbian centers may offer similar services.

• If you are on the street, school is probably the last thing on your mind. But alternative schools may be helpful if you were having trouble at school before you ran away. Alternative schools offer small classes and often teach practical skills as well as academic classes. Research has shown that attending these schools can increase some teenagers' self-esteem, which makes it easier for them to take charge of other areas of their lives.

Tired, hungry, with two black eyes, and covered in bruises, Marlena hovered outside the doors of Covenant House for two hours. It was snowing, and she was wearing only a thin pair of sneakers and a light coat over her clothes.

"I stood there shivering for two hours. I was

A Covenant House shelter in New York City.

afraid to go in. I was afraid that they would ask me to leave. I didn't think I had a right to anything. I didn't think I could ask for help.

"I did finally go in. I had to go up to the reception desk and ask them for something. But I didn't know what I wanted, I just didn't want to be out here anymore. I didn't want to be hit, or screwed, or raped. They were so kind. There was a counselor who hugged me. It was the first time I could remember being hugged."

If you are living on the streets, do not be afraid to look for help. Shelters are required by law to try to reunite children with their parents, but if this is not appropriate, they work with teens to find an alternative.

Talking to a trusted adult about your problems is an important first step in getting off the streets.

Many young people who have been away for only a short time return home wiser and more appreciative of home.

But not everyone can go home. In Los Angeles, only 20 percent of runaways actually return home and in New York, even fewer—less than 10 percent—return. Many of those who don't return are runaways who have been away from home for some time. Thirty-five percent of these teenagers do not even know where their parents can be contacted. If you cannot or do not want to go home, you are not alone. There are valid reasons why you and many others cannot return.

Not all children choose to run away.

Some are "throwaways" who are unwanted at home. Some parents do not want their children back after they have run away.

If you do return home, you may find that the situation you ran from has not changed. Without counseling, parents will probably have the same problems as before. If you ran away from alcoholism, drug abuse, or physical or sexual abuse, parents and children need counseling to be re-established as a family, or they will be back in the same situation.

If you do not know who to turn to, check out the Where to Go for Help section. The organizations listed all specialize in solving the problems that concern you.

"I stayed at Covenant House," says Marlena. "I went back to school. They placed me with foster parents who love me, and I'm doing well. They helped me quit drugs and showed me that there was more to life than hustling. It hasn't been an easy adjustment, but I'm starting to believe in myself—to believe that I have a right to be happy."

Glossary

addiction A physical or psychological need for a substance, such as a drug.

AIDS **(acquired immunodeficiency syndrome)** A fatal, incurable disease that is caused by the HIV virus and affects the immune system.

brothel A house or other building where prostitutes sell their services.

chicken hawk A man who pays for sex with a young male prostitute, or "chicken."

HIV **(human immunovirus)** The virus that causes AIDS.

hustler A slang term for a prostitute, especially a male prostitute.

john A man who pays for sex with a prostitute.

madam A woman who sells the services of prostitutes to customers, especially in a brothel, and keeps most of the money the prostitutes earn.

pimp Someone who sells the services of a prostitute to customers, usually men, and keeps most of the money the prostitutes earn.

prostitute A person who has sex or performs sexual acts for money.

STD **(sexually transmitted disease)** A disease that is given from one person to another through intercourse or other types of sexual contact.

throwaway A young person who has run away from home and whose parents do not want him or her to return.

Where to Go for Help

**Alcohol Hotline (Alcoholics
    Anonymous/Alanon/Alateen)**
(800) ALCOHOL [252-6465]

Children of the Night Hotline
(800) 551-1300

Cocaine Hotline
(800) COCAINE [262-2463]

Covenant House "Nine Line"
(800) 999-9999

Hetrick-Martin Institute
2 Astor Place
New York, NY 10003
(212) 674-2400

National AIDS Hotline
(800) 342-AIDS [342-2437]
Spanish: (800) 344-SIDA [344-7437]

National STD Hotline
(800) 227-8922

National Runaway Switchboard Crisis Line
(800) 621-4000

National Network of Runaway and Youth Services
400 I Street NW, Suite 300
Washington, DC 20004
(202) 783-7949

60 | **Project Connect and Youth Enrichment Services (Lesbian and Gay Community Services)**
208 West 13th Street
New York, NY 10011
(212) 620-7310

Prostitutes Anonymous
(818) 905-2188

Teen Help Line (Canada)
(800) 668-6868

Youth Crisis Hotline
(800) HIT-HOME [448-4663]

YouthLink (Canada)
(416) 922-3335

Web sites:

AIDS Research and Information Center
http://www.critpath.org.aric

Bureau for At-Risk Youth
http://www.at-risk.com

Condoms 101
http://www.umich.edu/~wespin/old-c101index.html

OutProud! The Coalition for Gay, Lesbian, and Bisexual Youth
http://www.youth.org/outproud

The STD Homepage
http://med-www.bu.edu/people/sycamore/std/std.htm

For Further Reading

Berger, Gilda. *Addiction.* New York: Franklin Watts, Inc., 1992.

Cheney, Glenn Alan. *Drugs, Teens, and Recovery: Real-Life Stories of Trying to Stay Clean.* Springfield, NJ: Enslow Publishers, Inc., 1993.

Dean, Ruth, and Melissa Thompson. *Teen Prostitution.* San Diego, CA: Lucent Books, 1997.

Glass, George. *Drugs and Fitting In.* New York: The Rosen Publishing Group, 1998.

Johnson, Joan J. *Teen Prostitution.* New York: Franklin Watts, Inc., 1992.

Plant, Martin, ed. *AIDS, Drugs, and Prostitution.* New York: Routledge, 1993.

Rawls, Bea O'Donnell, and Johnson, Gwen. *Drugs and Where to Turn.* New York: Rosen Publishing Group, 1993.

Video:
Teenage Runaways: Society's Children.

Index

About the Author

Clare Tattersall is a freelance writer. She writes plays, films, and magazine articles on a wide variety of topics. Her play *The Last Dance* was made into a short film. She lives in New York City.

Photo Credits